I am but mad north-north-west; when the wind is southerly, I know a hawk from a handsaw.

HAMLET. Act II, Scene 2

this book is pleased to belong to

TOOLC

carpenter in residence
JOSEPH KARSON

HEST

written, designed, and illustrated by

jan adkins

WALKER AND COMPANY

NEW YORK

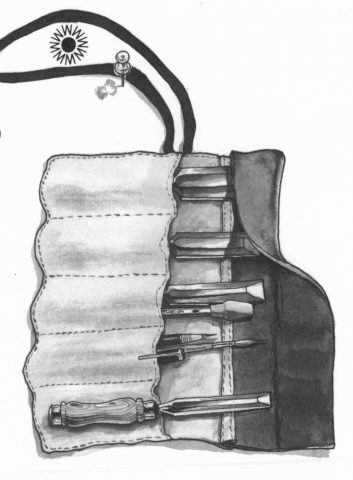

Every book should be dedicated to friends who are patient and loving, even to authors. This book is especially for fathers:

alban adkins   robert d. kiernan

the tree

The mechanism of a truly big tree encompasses a strange, still power that we six-foot, soft-fleshed, short-lived ground creatures cannot easily comprehend. The sawn board we buy for mere money at a lumber store is a cut out of life itself; a thin slice from a great tree that creaked in the wind, in whose branches birds and squirrels made their small lives, a great shelter, a food factory sucking water from the ground and sunlight from the day, a leafy, living mass. It is best to have respect and understanding for the wood we work.

ROOTS anchor a tree, spreading wider and deeper as the trunk and branches grow larger and demand more support. The roots absorb ground water with its dissolved minerals. Capillary action draws the water through the SAPWOOD of the trunk and branches, up and out to the leaves. Rough OUTER BARK is a tree's protection against blows, and a casing that encloses the moisture flowing within. The HEARTWOOD was once the sapwood of the young tree. Now outgrown, dead, darkened, and too dense to pass water upward, it is still part of the tree's great structural strength. In a process called photosynthesis, the leaves combine water, minerals from the soil, air, and sunlight to form sugars as food for the tree's life and growth. The sugars are passed back down along the branches and trunk through the INNER BARK and the MEDULLARY RAYS to feed the living cells of the sapwood and the CAMBIUM LAYER, an extremely thin sheath of cells growing outward by forming more sapwood. The cambium layer is the growing part of the tree. Its yearly cycle of quick growth during the spring and slower, darker growth during the summer forms concentric growth rings—one ring for each year of the tree's life.

If you work in wood, you will fill your mind with those rings, for they are every wood's strength, every wood's weakness, every wood's beauty. When a board is cut out of a tree trunk, the growth rings appear as patterns of lines and shadings on the board's surface, patterns called GRAIN.

7

grain

Grain shows itself on every piece of wood in three ways—three ways of looking at the growth rings: END GRAIN shows the end view of the growth rings, the ends of the long fibres that drew water up through the sapwood like thin straws, a circular, concentric pattern; SIDE GRAIN shows the fibres side by side, upright in the tree's trunk, fairly straight and generally parallel; FACE GRAIN shows a pattern made by the growth rings as they pass in and out of the flat plane made by the saw cut, a broad and meandering pattern of curves and smooth shadings. KNOTS are circular or oval irregularities coming out of the face grain. They are like tubes of darker, harder wood passing through the growth rings and are the overgrown beginnings of the young tree's branches that were buried in the later layers of the older tree. The darker medullary rays, the feeding routes that brought sugars into the sapwood from the inner bark, can form distinct grain patterns in some kinds of wood. If you think carefully about grain and growth rings, you can look at a piece of lumber and know how it lay in its parent tree.

In the late summer, the cambium layer of most trees grows very slowly, producing the tough, dark, dense part of the growth ring. The rapid spring growth is softer and less dense. A piece of wood, then, is composed of alternating layers of tough material and soft material. This structure of strong sheets sandwiched between light filler makes wood unusually light for its strength, and gives any piece of wood three qualities, depending on how the grain is used.

Think of a yardstick or a popsicle stick. Pressure on the flat surface bends it easily, but it stiffly resists bending from the side. A board is made up of many layers of growth rings that bend easily along the "flat" side (the face grain) but resist bending along their side grain.

If wood is used with pressure on its FACE GRAIN, it will be springy and resilient. If wood is used with pressure on its SIDE GRAIN, it will be stiff and strong. END GRAIN is extremely strong in compression, and resists impact.

FACE   EDGE   END

8

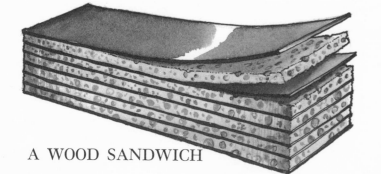

A WOOD SANDWICH

CUPPING

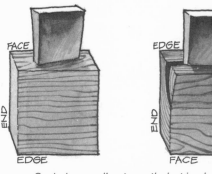

Grain is wood's strength, but is also its chief weakness. Because of the different qualities of the dense summer growth and lighter spring growth, wood must be used carefully, intelligently, to prevent several kinds of failure.

The light growth is weaker and will separate. If too great a strain is placed against face grain, beyond its ability to bend, it will split along the grain. If a wedge or cutting tool is driven too forcefully between the grain lines, the wood will split along the grain. Wood fibres separate easiest when parted at the end grain, and slivers or pieces can split off if a wedge is driven into the end grain. Grain in and around a knot is dense and confused. Cutting or shaping tools may dull quickly or nick when they are worked through knots. The knot itself is seldom well-attached to the entire piece of wood and may shrink and fall out (leaving a knothole), or it may cause the wood to break at that point.

Most woods are cured: they are rough cut and set to dry out in kilns or, better, over a long period of time in covered sheds. The light growth loses moisture at a different rate from the dense growth. This is a problem because wood fibers shrink when they lose moisture. The light growth shrinks more than the dense, and contracts along the grain sideways (it shrinks very little lengthwise). Since it is bonded very tightly to the dense grain, it deforms the whole piece, or CUPS it.

9

woods

There are as many woods as shadings of climate, thousands of varieties of trees spreading branches and sinking roots in almost every part of the world. Each wood has a unique set of qualities and working pecularities.

Lumbermen group all woods in two broad categories: softwoods and hardwoods. Softwoods are from coniferous trees (the pines, firs, spruces and hemlocks) and are resinous woods. Hardwoods are from the broad-leafed deciduous trees (maple, oak, walnut, etc.) and have little resin. For the woodcrafter, the categories have uncertain meaning since some softwoods are harder than some hardwoods. The woodcrafter wants to know how truly hard a wood is, how pronounced its grain, how heavy it is for its strength, how it finishes, how well it resists decay under various conditions. Today it is difficult and expensive to select many varieties of wood for specific uses, but the woodworkers of earlier America knew that everything they fashioned had a suitable wood.

A house carpenter might use five woods in a single door, and the shipwright a dozen woods for a small dinghy. If we can't choose among a hundred woods, we choose even more carefully among the scant twenty available. But a romance and a just-so sense are lost without all the old woods to handle.

✠	fairly strong
✠✠	very strong, structural use
⚓	unstable, decays easily
⚓ ⚓	stable in a protected environment
⚓ ⚓ ⚓	very stable, weather resistant
◉	relatively soft
◉◉	firm
◉◉◉	dense and very hard
⚒	difficult to work with
⚒⚒	requiring caution to work well
⚒⚒⚒	responsive and easy to work
☆	difficult to finish
☆☆	finishes fairly well
☆☆☆	yields a high finish

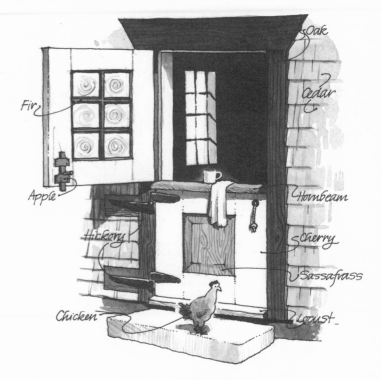

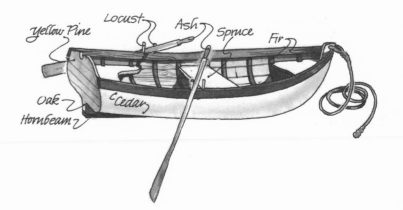

10

	strength	stability	hardness	workability	finish	uses
Ash	✹	⚓⚓	●●	⚒⚒	☆☆	tool handles, baseball bats, legs, chairs
Beech	✹	⚓⚓	●●	⚒⚒	☆☆	furniture, wooden tools
Birch	✹	⚓	●●	⚒⚒⚒	☆☆☆	tables, chairs, dowels
Cedar①	✹	⚓⚓⚓	●	⚒⚒⚒	☆☆	cabinetry, cigar boxes, closets
Cherry	✹✹	⚓⚓	●●●	⚒⚒⚒	☆☆☆	fine cabinetry and furniture
Chestnut	✹	⚓⚓	●●	⚒⚒	☆	chests, dressers
Elm	✹	⚓	●●	⚒⚒	☆	end-grain for butcher blocks, lowgrade furniture
Fir, Douglas and White②	✹✹	⚓⚓⚓	●●	⚒	☆	construction, structural timber
Gum	✹	⚓⚓	●●	⚒⚒	☆☆☆	table tops, dressers
Hickory	✹✹	⚓⚓	●●●	⚒	☆	chairs, handles
Mahogany	✹✹	⚓⚓⚓	●●	⚒⚒⚒	☆☆☆	marine trim, fine furniture, musical instruments
Maple	✹✹	⚓⚓	●●●	⚒⚒⚒	☆☆☆	chairs, tables, instruments
Oak	✹✹	⚓⚓	●●●	⚒⚒	☆	heavy furniture, structural
Pine, eastern white	✹	⚓⚓	●	⚒⚒⚒	☆☆	interior trim, utility trim
Pine, long leaf yellow	✹✹	⚓⚓⚓	●●	⚒⚒	☆☆	marine structural, heavy construction
Poplar	✹	⚓	●●	⚒⚒⚒	☆☆	cabinets, tables, panels, pianos
Redwood	✹	⚓⚓⚓	●	⚒⚒⚒	☆☆	exterior trim, exterior furnishing, construction
Rosewood③		⚓⚓⚓	●●●	⚒⚒⚒	☆☆☆	fine inlay, small boxes and cabinets
Spruce	✹✹	⚓⚓	●	⚒⚒	☆	sailing masts, musical instruments, canoe paddles
Sycamore	✹	⚓⚓⚓	●●●	⚒	☆☆	veneers, utility cabinets
Teak	✹✹	⚓⚓⚓	●●	⚒⚒	☆☆	marine uses, fine furniture, sitars
Walnut	✹✹	⚓⚓	●●	⚒⚒⚒	☆☆☆	fine cabinetry and furniture

① Many woods are called cedar, but the finish carpenter concerns himself almost exclusively with the hardwood cedar.

② Douglas fir and white fir are construction timbers, and their stability can only be judged in a structural sense, and not by the standards of the finish carpenter.

③ Rosewood is a rare and beautiful material used decoratively; it almost never bears load.

TOOLS

Man is the tool-using species because he is a thinking species, a dissatisfied and impatient species. He sees the world around him as imperfect, threatening to his comfort or his balance, and impatiently he shapes his world with the tools his mind can devise and his hands can fashion. He selects, rejects, replaces, reforms. What is most important is that he makes something new, something that exists only because he put his hand to it. That special creation is the joy of working by hand.

Few things in our lives today are hand-crafted, but there is still a bond between a worker and his tools that grows with use. If a worker's feeling for a long-used chisel or knife or hammer is not affection, it is at least a rare respect.

The beauty of simple tools stays with us. Few pieces of museum sculpture compare well with the curves of the farmer's sickle and scythe, the gleaming faces of a sharp chisel, or the angular rhythm of a sawblade. Their forms are shaped by the work they do and the hands that guide them. They have a clean look of function and directness.

The workman and his tools produce something beyond what is useful or saleable. Together they accomplish pride and art. In a time not so long ago when one craftsman was largely responsible for building an entire home, several master carpenters presented their toolchests to a prospective client. He inspected their tools: the newness of the edges and the wear of the handles, the art of wood-joining in the chests, the strength of the joints, the cleverness of construction. The client chose a carpenter by the condition of his tools; it told him something about the way tools and craftsman worked together.

Working in wood is an exact sort of thing. The parts of a piece should join nicely, tightly, as if they had grown just that way. The woodcrafter uses his tapes and rules as guides only, preferring to match one part against another. A rule of thumb: Measure as little as possible.

measuring tools

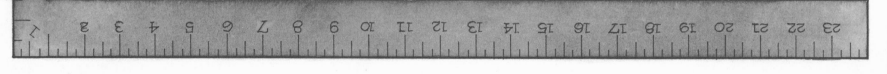

BLADE

BEAM

FRAMING SQUARE

TRYSQUARE

Two of the most important measuring tools are the TRYSQUARE and the FRAMING SQUARE. They are both used to lay out or test a right angle (90°, the angle of a square's four corners). To TRY a board is to set its faces and edges at right angles to one another by sawing or planing, and the trysquare measures right angles to follow. Its overlapping BEAM can be slid along a

board's edge and a right angle can be marked along the BLADE, all around the board if necessary. The larger framing square is used to check the overall relation of parts, to check outside angles, or to mark boards too broad for the trysquare. (Whole books have been written on the many uses of the framing square as a guide for measuring and laying out angles.)

The folding wooden rule is the old carpenter's favorite, and it has the advantage of being fairly rigid when moved about. It should not be used face down, but on edge for best accuracy. The tape rule is more compact and in some ways handier. Six inches of one is half a foot of the other.

In marking a point to be drilled or nailed, a lead pencil or a colored pencil

MARKING GAUGE   MARKING KNIFE

head

is fine; but in marking an extremely ac-
curate line, or a line to be sawn or
chiseled, a MARKING KNIFE is better.
A pencil line varies slightly as the point
wears or the pencil is turned, but a fine,
shallow cut with a flat-sided knife is
constant. If a line is SCRIBED, or scored
deeply, before sawing or chiseling, the
cut guides the tool and prevents a
ragged edge.

MARKING GAUGES are used to
scribe a line along an edge. The dis-
tance between the HEAD and the CUT-
TER is set with a rule and held with the
thumbscrew. The face of the head is held
firmly against the edge of the board and
is drawn along it.

cutting tools: saws

To cut clean and true is the first skill of the woodworker. The correctness of measurement and angle in sawing is called the *truth* of the cut, and is decided by the first stroke of the saw, just as this first, basic skill often decides the truth and quality of the entire project.

RIP TEETH   CROSSCUT TEETH

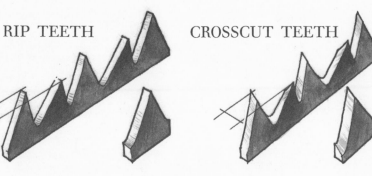

Look closely at the sawblade. There are hundreds of small teeth—not in line, but bent out of line, alternately right and left. If the saw is sharp, each tooth is like a tiny chisel. As the sawblade is thrust through the wood, each of these chisels gouges away a bit of wood and carries it out of the grooves made by the cut. The degree to which the teeth are bent right and left out of line is called the SET of the teeth; the set makes the groove cut by the saw (called the KERF) wider than the blade so the saw will not stick in its own cut. The set also provides a kind of cargo space between the teeth for the bits of cut wood being carried

out of the kerf.

There are two saw categories: RIP SAWS and CROSSCUT SAWS. Rip saws cut best with the grain; that is, parallel to the side grain. A rip saw is used to cut down the length of a board. Its teeth are sharpened straight across the blade.

Crosscut saws are used for cutting across the grain—sawing a board off to size, for instance. A utility crosscut saw has a medium set and 8 to 12 teeth per inch. The teeth of a crosscut saw are sharpened at an angle to the blade, so they are more like slanting knives than squareface chisels.

When this 2x6 is measured, the carpenter scribes a deep line with trysquare and marking knife, across the face and down the far edge. These marks will guide him horizontally. To guide his first strokes vertically, he rests his trysquare upright on its beam, directly beside the scribed line. He has pencilled "G" on the measured side and "W" on the other side of the line—"G" for "Good" and "W" for "Waste." If he measures several pieces at once he could forget on which side of the line to saw, and the resulting piece would be shorter by the width of the kerf (the saw cut). He could clamp the 2x6 to the workbench, but in this case, sawing it on a low bench, he is kneeling on the board to steady it. Using his thumb to guide the blade, he starts the kerf with a slow backstroke to "set" the blade. Notice the grip: extending the index finger along the side of the handle helps to direct the stroke. Guided ver-

tically by the trysquare, he makes the first part of the cut at a shallow angle, carefully following the scribed line. After a few strokes, the saw is brought up to its normal angle (40° to 45° for a crosscut saw, 60° to 65° for a ripsaw) and he carefully follows the line on the far edge of the board. Remember that the first strokes are the most important part of the cut, that once the kerf is deep enough to hold the blade, the direction of the cut is committed. He saws with regular, easy strokes, pressing down and into the cut, but not forcing it. The return stroke is relaxed, since the saw does not cut in that direction. He uses his extended index finger to feel the direction. The trysquare can be removed now, and when the piece is sawn nearly through, he holds the waste piece steady with his left hand to prevent splitting at the bottom of the kerf.

BACKSAW

The BACKSAW is for precise work. It has fine teeth (12 to 16 per inch) and a narrow set. Its name comes from a stiff spine along the back of its blade that prevents bending. The toothed side of the blade is parallel to the back, because the backsaw is often used to cut level to a certain depth, and the woodworker uses the back to gauge the levelness of the cut. It is stroked horizontally except for the starting cuts. The backsaw is often used with a mitre box or a bench hook.

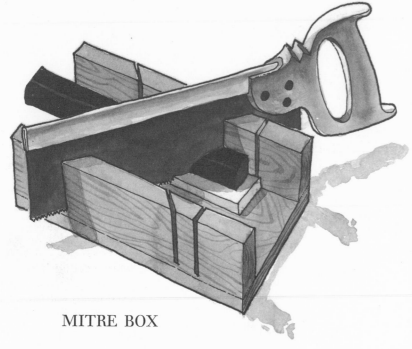

MITRE BOX

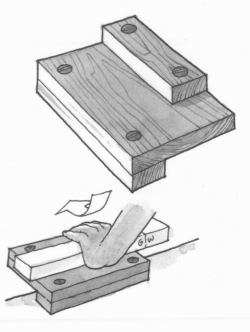

BENCH HOOK

The MITRE BOX is used to cut angles. Some mitre boxes are adjustable to any angle, but most are simple wooden boxes with slots to guide a saw in cutting a 45° angle (the angle that will join two boards at a 90°) or a "square" angle (90°). The piece to be cut is clamped or held very tightly against the side of the box and down against a scrap piece on the bottom of the box. The backsaw is guided by the slots, cutting through the piece and into the scrap.

The BENCH HOOK is an old carpenter's tool. It is used to hold a small piece to be sawn. The lower lip is hooked against the edge of a bench or table, and the piece is pushed firmly into the notch made by the upper lip.

18

The COPING SAW has a thin, narrow blade held in tension. It is used to cut complex shapes in thin stock because the slender blade can turn within its own kerf. A coping blade has very fine teeth, sometimes reversed so that they cut on the backstroke rather than on the forestroke, as most saws do. The backstroke is not as powerful as the forestroke, but it can be more controllable. The coping saw can be used to cut interior shapes if the blade is detached, threaded through a drilled hole, and reattached for cutting inside the piece.

The BOW SAW is used for cutting shapes in heavy wood.

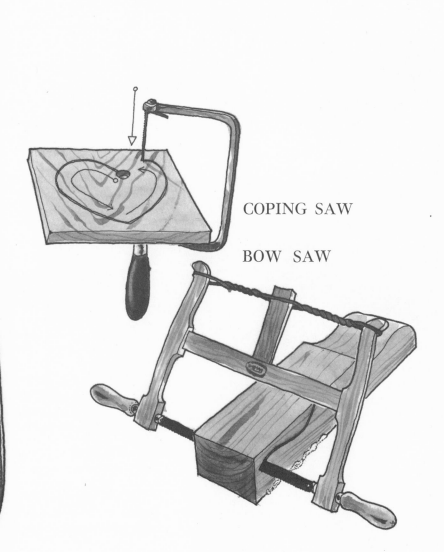

COPING SAW

BOW SAW

19

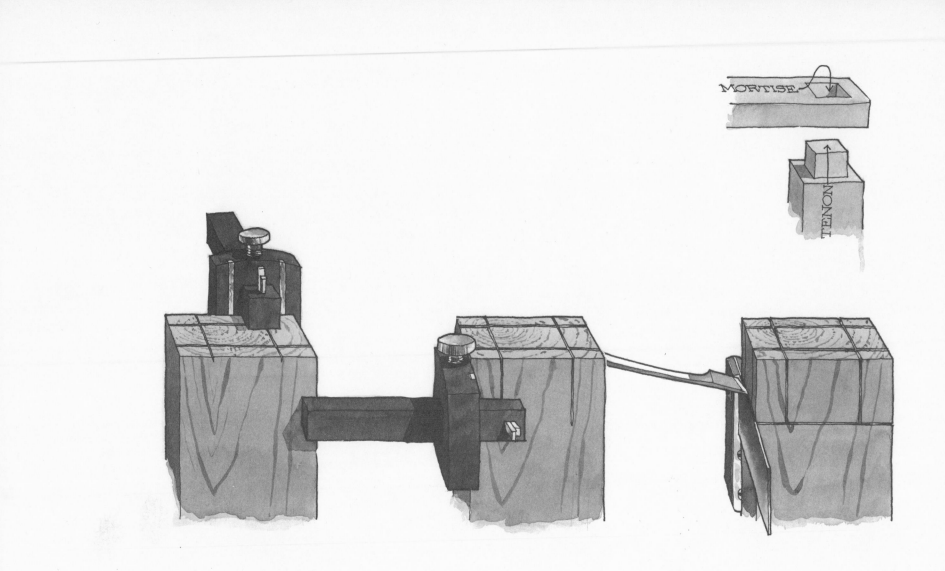

A TENON and a MORTISE go together, as a way to join two pieces. The
mortise is a hole, precisely cut in one
piece, that accepts the precisely cut end
of another piece, the tenon. The mortise
is chiseled out, but the tenon is usually
sawn with a backsaw. For the tenon, the
end of this 4 x 4 is scribed with a mark-

20

ing gauge, and the lines run down the sides with a trysquare or a marking gauge to guide the saw cut. The depth line is marked all around with the trysquare. The first cuts are made down from the top, into end grain. The kerf is begun along the top scribe, and the saw is then tipped up to begin it along the side. The kerf beginnings on end and side tend to hold the saw to a true cut. The backsaw, held horizontally, cuts down to the depth lines. When all four end cuts have been made, the side cuts (or shoulder cuts) free the waste pieces and the tenon is ready.

shaping tools: chisels

The chisel is a crude tool that can be used with delicacy and even precision. It is little more than a strong blade with a handle to guide it; the wedge of its blade cuts and lifts the waste out of the way to shape and fashion wood. The wedge and the edge are the two parts of the most ancient tools: axes, adzes, and chisels. However crude and ancient the chisel may be, when it is razor sharp in skilled hands it still produces the most complex and refined woodcraft.

THE THREE CHISEL types begin with the most basic, the MORTISE CHISEL, with flat edges and surface. It is used as a chopping tool to cut away chunks of waste, and it is struck with a wooden mallet (not a steel hammer). The mortise chisel usually has a socket handle, a steel cup into which the handle fits; when the handle is struck, it is compressed into the cup even tighter.

THE PARING CHISEL, also called the cabinet chisel, is thinner, has a bevelled face, and is used by hand to shave away rough irregularities and to "clean up" after the mortise chisel. It most often has a tang handle: a steel shaft from the blade fitting into a hole drilled in the handle. Bashing this kind of handle with a mallet would tend to split it open.

A GOUGE is essentially a sculptor's tool used to cut grooves or sculpt in wood Sculptors strike their large gouge with round-headed mauls rather than flat-faced mallets; concentrating properly on the cutting edge of their tool, and not on the end to be struck, the face of a mallet might not strike the gouge squarely, and might deflect it from its path. All careful chiselers concentrate on the cut and let their hands do the striking.

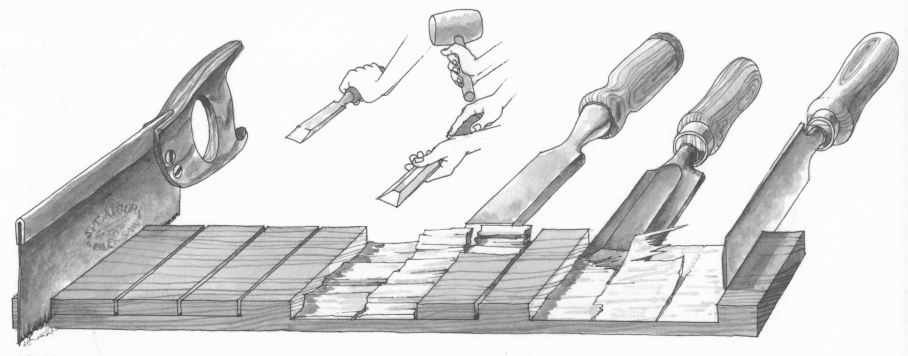

Careful thought about grain
is essential to chiseling.
ALWAYS CHISEL UPHILL is a solid rule. Wood splits
along its grain; if you chisel ''downhill'' as at the left,
the chisel is wedging the grain apart and will split the
piece. Chiseling ''uphill'', on the right here, the chisel
cuts across the grain and the splitting tendency helps lift the waste out.

A DADO is a slot cut to accept another piece that is to be joined at that point. Using a try square and marking knife on the face, and using a marking gauge along the edge, the dado is laid out and scribed. A backsaw makes the edge cuts and additional cuts inside the dado, all to correct depth.

Working uphill, the mortise chisel is held horizontally to chop out most of the waste. (A block might be clamped to the side away from the chisel to prevent chipping below the deeply scribed depth-line.)

The paring chisel, hand-held and horizontal, shaves away the remaining waste. It is also used to clean up the sides of the dado, held on edge.

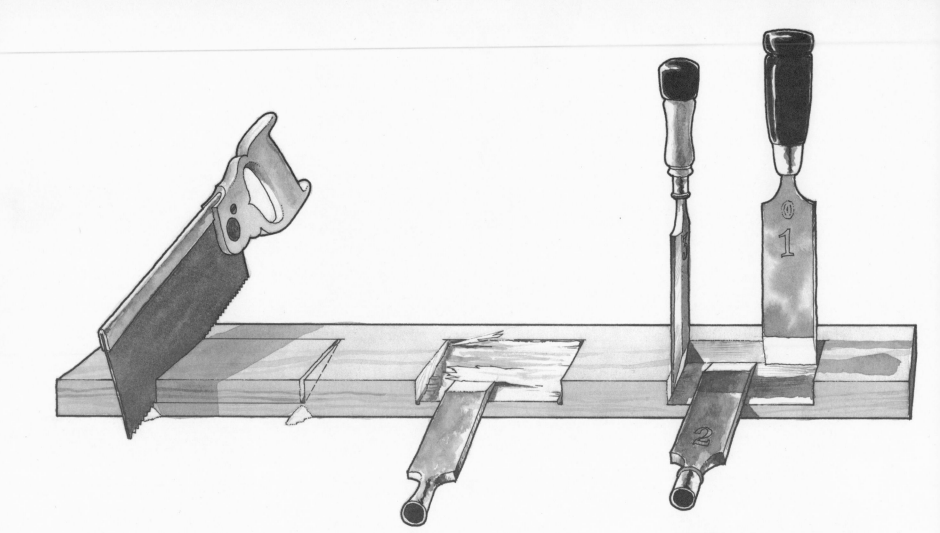

A STOPPED MORTISE is made when the notch does not cut into both edges, but stops somewhere between. Saw cuts are made, as they are with a dado; but they are made at an angle, from the line scribed on the edge to the line on the face. Remember to clamp your piece securely before chiseling, so you can work on a steady surface. Because the chisel is a wedge, its flat side

is pushed away from the bevelled side. Rather than have the marked edge marred by the flat side "backing up," you can begin about 1/16" away from the scribed line, cutting down into face grain a little and lifting the waste away with a cut into the side grain. Use a chisel as big as possible; a wider chisel cuts cleaner and its broad, flat surface guides the cut. Below the saw cuts you

will have to cut the sides of the mortise, chiseling three ways: down at both sides of the mortise, down again at the back, and then in from the open end of the mortise to cut and lift out the waste. When the mortise is roughed out, you can pare back to the scribed lines (you may want to refresh the edge of your chisel before you begin paring) and the edges of the mortise will be clean.

A BLIND MORTISE doesn't interrupt either edge. The mortise is marked and scribed, and an auger (see page 33) is used to drill out most of the waste inside it. If the mortise goes all the way through the board, the rest of the waste is chopped cleanly through with a mortise chisel, mallet-driven down into a scrap board clamped under the working piece. If the mortise stops part of the way

through, auger out the waste (using a bit of string or piece of tape around the auger bit to gauge the proper depth), and chisel in at an angle, beginning a little way from the mortise's edge so it will not be marred and rounded when you pry out the waste. When the bottom is satisfactorily cleared, pare the sides out to size.

planes

Geometrically, a plane is a flat surface. To the woodworker, a plane is a tool for shaping a flat, smooth surface. It is a refining instrument, a tool of delicacy. The plane is the difference between rough construction and finish carpentry.

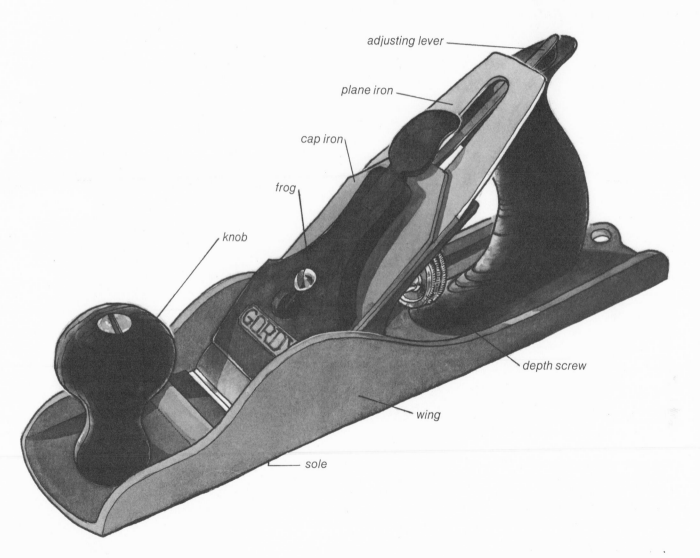

adjusting lever

plane iron

cap iron

frog

knob

depth screw

wing

sole

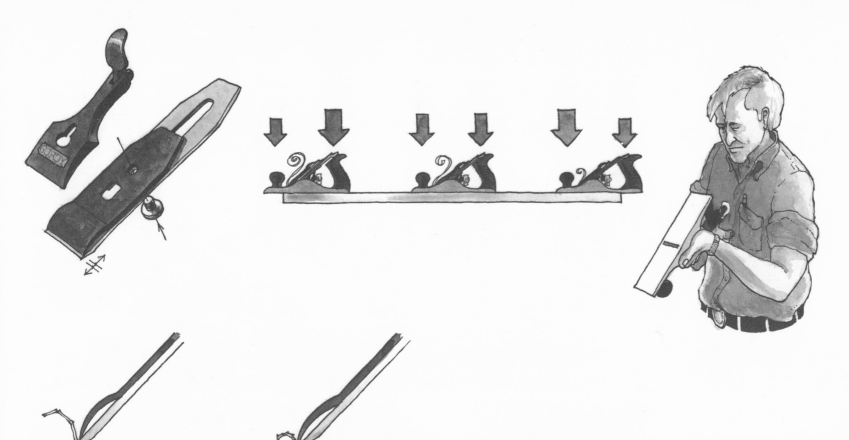

A JACK PLANE is the basic planing tool, and becoming acquainted with it is basic carpentry. Essentially, a plane is a device for holding a chisel at a precise angle and depth, in order to shave thin slices of wood from the piece. The cutting blade—called the iron—is clamped into the plane, extending through a slot in the bottom, or sole. The depth to which the iron extends is adjusted by the screw under the iron, and the depth de-cides the thickness of the slice—the curl—the plane takes. As the depth of the cut is adjusted, the CAP IRON should be adjusted, too. The cap iron is the plate clamped on the back of the cutting iron; its purpose is to make the cutting iron more rigid and to break the curl as it is cut from the surface, so that the blade doesn't wedge out splinters of grain deeper than its cut. The cap iron is set close to the edge for fine, shallow cutting, and

further back for rough, deeper planing. The depth screw can be set up and down, but the final adjustment should be down, so the iron bears against the screw and will not slip back into the sole.

It is critical to the evenness of the curl that the blade's edge be parallel to the sole. The adjusting lever, shifted right and left while you sight down the sole, tilts the blade until it is parallel.

A plane is given a long and

smooth stroke, with the grain and "uphill," bearing heaviest on the foregrip at the beginning of the stroke, heaviest on the backgrip toward the end of the stroke, evenly in the middle. This shifting of weight helps to offset a tendency to cut deeper into the ends and leave the middle higher. Like a chisel, the plane should always cut uphill and with the grain.

27

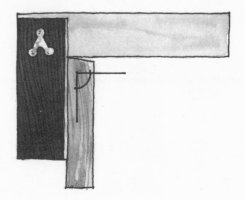

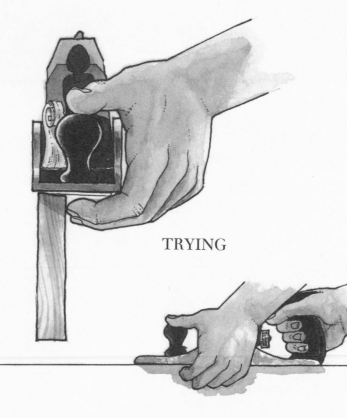

TRYING

The jack plane's name comes from its versatility: it is used to "hog" rough stock (bring it down to proper dimensions), to smooth surfaces, to straighten and try edges. Used to TRY (or true) the edges of a board, the plane is held with the forward hand curled over the wing (the side) of the plane, fingers grazing the face of the board to "feel" the angle between edge and face. The plane is stroked in the direction of the board's edge, but if the board is narrow

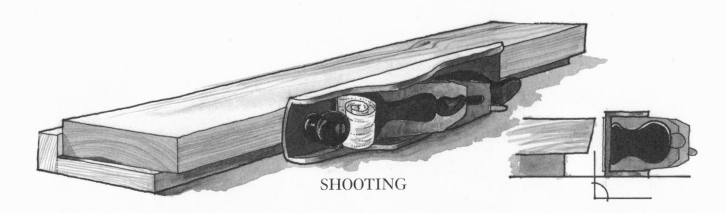

SHOOTING

it is held at an angle to use more of the blade's width.

SHOOTING an edge is another, more positive, method of trying. The piece is clamped flat on a workbench, raised by a thin piece beneath it. The plane is laid on its wing and stroked along the board's edge, depending on the right angle between sole and wing to form a right angle between edge and face. Some planes are fitted with a handle socket on the side to aid in shooting. With either method, the angle can be checked with a trysquare, and the straightness with a metal or wood straightedge.

The relative flatness of a surface can be checked with WYNDING LATHS: two trued lengths of hard, stable wood—one with a dark top, the other with a light top. Placing them on the surface and sighting across their top edges, the woodworker can detect even slight variations in the board's flatness, or WYND.

WYNDING BOARDS

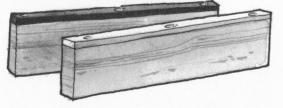

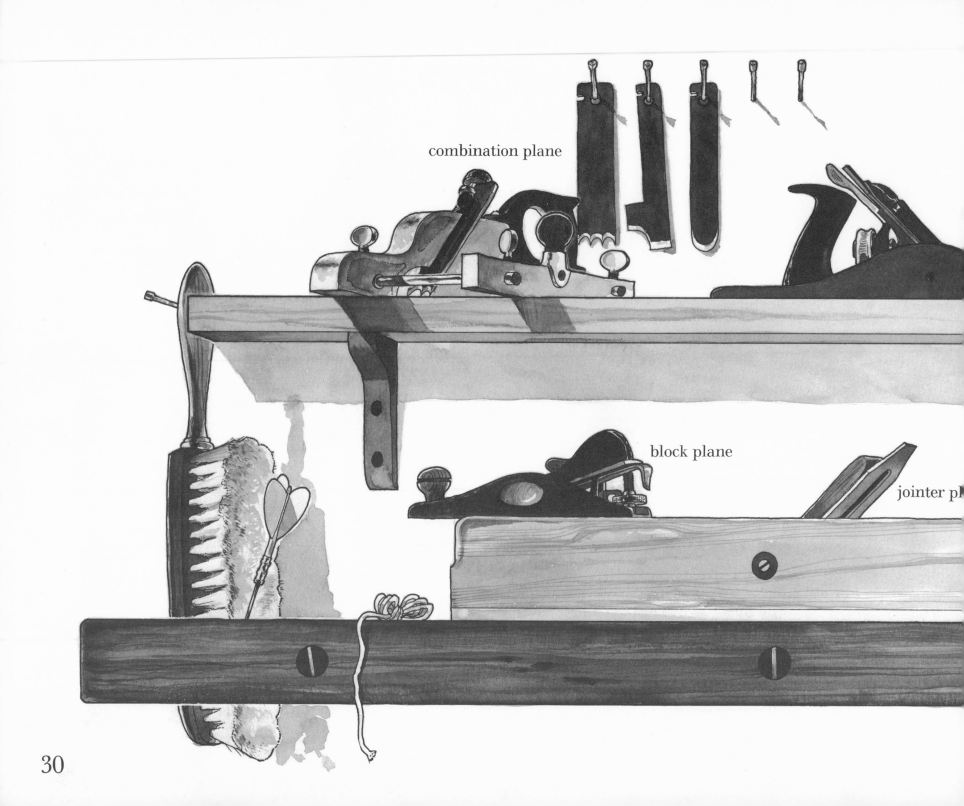

combination plane

block plane

jointer pl

30

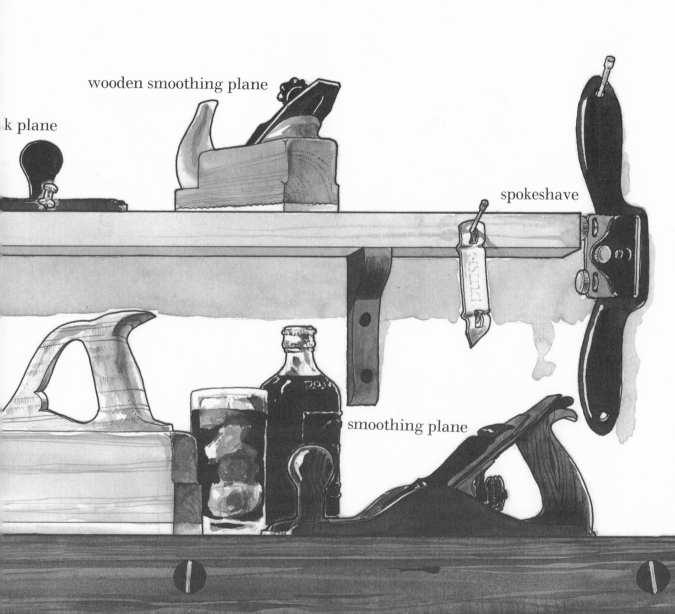

k plane

wooden smoothing plane

spokeshave

smoothing plane

There are two other types of bench planes. The JOINTER PLANE has a longer sole to assure a truer cut. It is set fine and used for precise trying of edges and surfaces, especially for joining pieces of wood edge to edge. The SMOOTHING PLANE is shorter than the jack plane and is used to finish surfaces smooth.

The BLOCK PLANE is specifically for planing end grain. It was once used to resurface the end grain tops of chopping blocks. Its iron is set—without a cap—at a shallow angle that is less apt to tear the wood. It is shorter and has no wooden handle for the back hand. Because end grain splits off easily at the sides, the strokes should be made from the sides toward the middle, when possible, or a block should be clamped on the side away from the stroke. The block plane is sometimes used as a jack plane when there is no vise, since it can be used one-handed.

The SHAPING PLANES use shaped blades to cut forms and grooves. They take many forms, some for finishing the bottoms and sides of mortises, some for cutting moldings or ploughing grooves.

The SPOKESHAVE is a small two-handled plane drawn toward the user to shave smaller, rounded pieces. At one time it was used to shape the tapering spokes of wooden coach wheels.

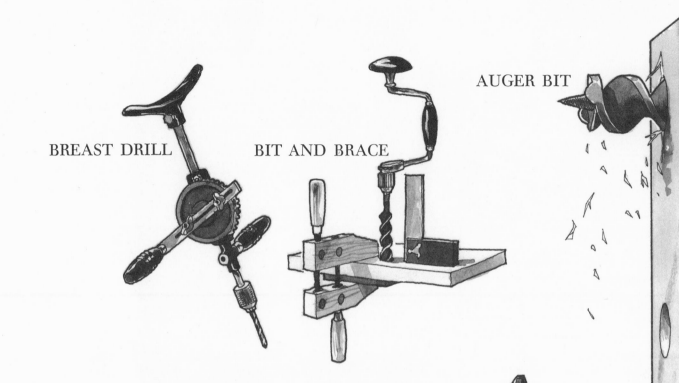

BREAST DRILL

BIT AND BRACE

AUGER BIT

TWIST BIT

DRILL POINT

boring tools

Making a straight, deep hole is not easy. Shipwrights and barn-builders once tended charcoal fires beside their hulls and frames to heat bundles of steel rods white hot. A rod was plucked from the sparkling heat with long tongs and driven into the ribs or beams, burning a hole. Later craftsmen designed some of the cleverest and most specialized tools we have to do the same, necessary job.

A TWIST BIT is designed for smaller holes, higher speeds. It is used in a geared HAND DRILL (the eggbeater model) or the larger BREAST DRILL.

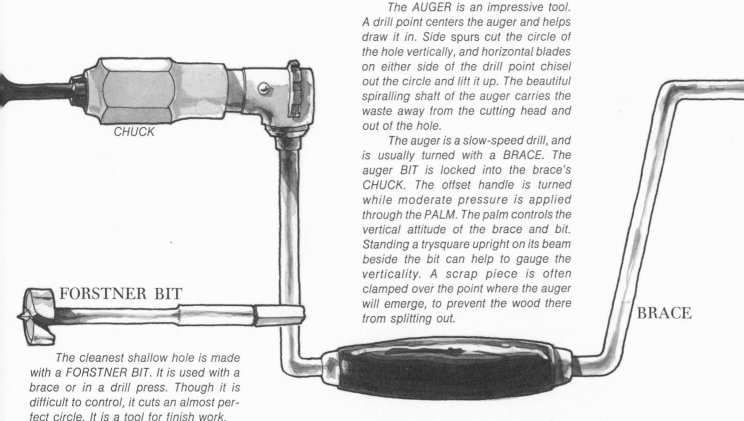

CHUCK

FORSTNER BIT

The cleanest shallow hole is made with a FORSTNER BIT. It is used with a brace or in a drill press. Though it is difficult to control, it cuts an almost perfect circle. It is a tool for finish work.

The AUGER is an impressive tool. A drill point centers the auger and helps draw it in. Side spurs cut the circle of the hole vertically, and horizontal blades on either side of the drill point chisel out the circle and lift it up. The beautiful spiralling shaft of the auger carries the waste away from the cutting head and out of the hole.

The auger is a slow-speed drill, and is usually turned with a BRACE. The auger BIT is locked into the brace's CHUCK. The offset handle is turned while moderate pressure is applied through the PALM. The palm controls the vertical attitude of the brace and bit. Standing a trysquare upright on its beam beside the bit can help to gauge the verticality. A scrap piece is often clamped over the point where the auger will emerge, to prevent the wood there from splitting out.

BRACE

PALM

PUSH DRILL

BIGELOW

The PUSH DRILL is for more casual work, like screw and brad holes. It cuts with a DRILL POINT that is turned by a spring-loaded gear as the handle is pushed.

dowelling

Joining wood to wood with a bit of wood has a sense of balance for the woodworker. It seemed consistent and thrifty to a carpenter of the old times. He called dowels "trunnels" or "treenails." Though the dowel is, on one hand, a simple cylinder, it is also a subtle and strong holdfast.

A dowel seldom works alone. Rather than support a load by itself, it most often fixes the position of a piece in a mortise or groove, allowing the mortise to withstand most of the strain. It might be used to fix a tenon in a through-mortise or to secure a length of stock in a stopped-mortise.

The principle of the dowel is simple, and the procedure for setting dowels is not much more difficult. Two pieces are placed together and a common hole is drilled through them. A wooden pin (the dowel) is fitted snugly into the hole and the pieces are bound—in one plane at least. Both the dowel and the pieces joined are glued, and the dowel is sometimes wedged to secure its own position.

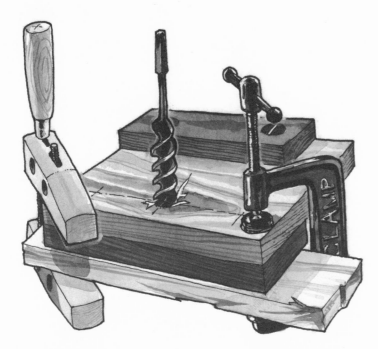

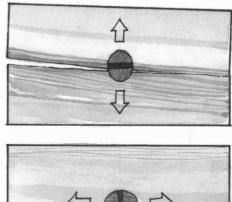

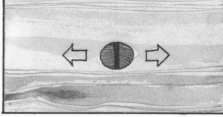

This BENCH HOOK is to be fastened with dowels so no metal screws or nails will dull saw teeth. The pieces are clamped together and ⅜" holes are bored through both. Two ⅜" dowels are cut, about ½" longer than necessary to pass through both pieces. Lengths of dowelling are available for this purpose. At one time oak, elm and locust dowels were favored. The dowels are slotted at their ends to receive wedges, and this requires some careful thought. When a wedge is driven into a dowel's end, the end is expanded against the surrounding wood, and this tightness keeps the dowel in place. Do not forget, though that the wedge is a powerful machine—more powerful than the bond between the growth rings of the lumber. If the wedge causes the dowel to expand in a direction that separates the grain, it will almost certainly split the piece. Make sure the dowel expands against end grain, rather than between the grain. When a dowel fastens two pieces with different grain directions, it may even be necessary to cut the wedge slots at different angles. The slots are cut with a backsaw, deeper than the wedges by about ⅛".

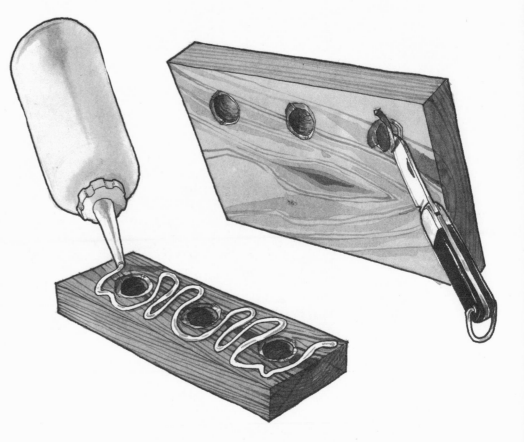

The ends to be driven in are chamfered: the edges are removed with a knife or file to seat the dowel without marring the edge of the dowel-hole. A spiral groove is also cut along the length of the dowel with a knife or the edge of a file; this equalizes the fluid pressure of the glue inside the hole.

The pieces to be joined are unclamped and taken apart to be glued.

Spread the wood glue evenly over all the parts that touch. It is also a good practice to cut around the edges of the auger holes on the interior faces (again, to allow for glue pressure). Rejoin the pieces and clamp them, spread the dowel with a coat of glue, and seat them lightly so that their wedge slots are at the proper angle to the grains of both pieces.

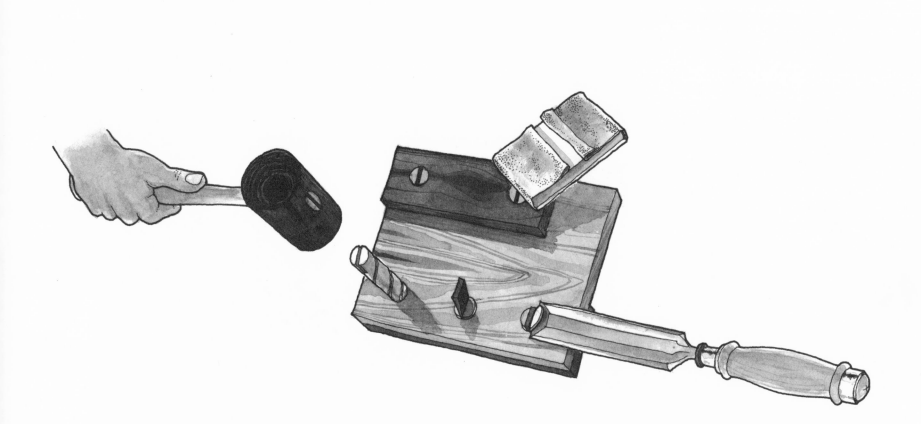

Before you drive the dowels, remember that each one must be driven continuously with firm, square, uninterrupted blows. If you stop for more than a second or two the dowel will sieze and may refuse to be driven further. Use a wooden mallet, and drive until the dowel is almost level with the surface.

The wedges must be of a dense, strong wood: oak is excellent. They are whittled or cut or filed to the width of the dowel and a thickness that will slightly expand the slot. Seat them carefully and tap them all the way in with square, well-placed blows. When the wedges are driven, the dowel ends can be cut level with a chisel, then sanded smooth.

nails

The nail is a brave tool. It is beaten into a depth of wood with a heavy blunt instrument—a violent facet of woodworking.

Essentially, the nail is a metal dowel, making its own hole and wedging itself. Like the dowel, the nail in most cases should not supply strength, but hold strength in place; that is, the construction of the project you are making—its mortises and joints—should withstand the main strain, and nails should only hold the parts of the project in place. A nail resists strain across itself but holds poorly against a strain pulling it directly out of its hole.

The construction carpenter and the finish carpenter view nails differently. The construction carpenter's nails are thick and big-headed, driven with a heavy hand and a heavy 18 or 20 ounce hammer. The finish carpen-

ter seems embarrassed to be using nails, and slyly brings thin nails without heads, which he sinks about 1/8" below the surface with a NAILSET and a 13 ounce hammer.

The finish carpenter, for all his reluctance, has several tricks with nails. To give the face of his hammer head a better "hold" on the nail head, and to avoid its slipping off to one side, he taps the face with the edge of a rasp-file, giving it a pocked texture that "grips" better. The finish carpenter uses hard woods more often than the construction carpenter, and the danger of splitting hardwood is greater. A pilot hole is often drilled in hardwood to prevent splitting, slightly smaller than the diameter of

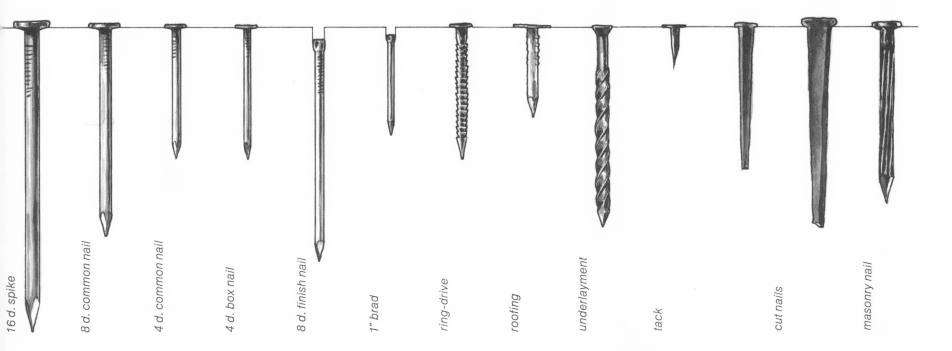

16 d. spike

8 d. common nail

4 d. common nail

4 d. box nail

8 d. finish nail

1" brad

ring-drive

roofing

underlayment

tack

cut nails

masonry nail

the nail. When a nail must be driven near an edge or end, the piece is clamped before drilling a pilot hole or driving. A pilot hole may be unnecessary if the tip of the nail is bulled, or blunted by tapping it with the hammer. (This does not seem especially logical, but it seems to work.)

Give a nail a chance, and it will bend. Keeping your hammer face clean and grease free will help keep the nail true, and so will an easy hammer swing from your whole arm—shoulder, elbow and wrist—that brings the face flat to the nail head. When a nail bends, though, you must remove it and try again. Slip a piece of scrap between the hammer back and the wood before you begin to draw the

nail out, and increase the height of the claw with another bit of scrap to draw the bent nail further. The increasing height gives you better leverage and draws the nail straighter, so the wood around the nail hole is not marred.

There are many nail patterns for specific jobs. Nail sizes are gauged in pennies, a measurement from old England that probably indicated the number of nails in a certain weight, or perhaps how many nails could be bought for a pence. "Pennies" is usually abbreviated, so a four penny nail (about 1½" long) is written 4 d. The "d." stands for denarius, a Latin word for "coin." An 8 d. nail is about 2½" long, and a 16 d. spike is about

3½". Construction nails, or COMMON NAILS have wide, flat heads. BOX NAILS are for crating; they are thinner, so as not to split thin crate wood, and they are cheaper than common nails, but also weaker. FINISH NAILS are slender, headless nails with a dimple in the top to hold the punch or nailset used to sink them. BRADS are very small finish nails. RING-DRIVE NAILS have raised rings the length of their shafts; the planks of a boat's hull are often attached to its ribs with ring-shanked nails made of bronze, monel, or another weather-resistant metal. ROOFING NAILS are short, thick, galvanized nails for attaching tar-paper to roof sheathing. UNDERLAYMENT NAILS, used to se-

cure subflooring, have raised, twisting ridges the length of their shafts, and turn as they are driven in. Sharp TACKS hold upholstery, carpeting, canvas, or leather to wood. CUT NAILS are cut from flat bar stock, the oldest style of nails. MASONRY NAILS are tempered (hardened) to be driven into concrete block, mortar, or brick, and are often used to fasten wood to the masonry foundations of a house.

The basic machines are the wedge, the lever, the wheel, and the screw. Among them, the most powerful is the screw. A screw is man's mind multiplying the efforts of his muscles.

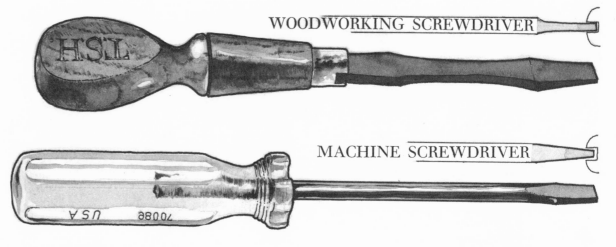

WOODWORKING SCREWDRIVER

MACHINE SCREWDRIVER

screws

A SCREW is a wedge wrapped around a cylinder. If you cut a paper wedge and wrap it around a pencil, you will see the spiralling screw pattern it makes. A MACHINE SCREW (or BOLT) has its shallow ridges (threads) wrapped around a straight cylinder. A metal NUT is cut to accept the threads so that it turns up and down on them. A hole is drilled, the machine screw is slipped through it, and the nut is screwed tight over a round plate called a WASHER and the pieces to be held.

Woodworkers use the WOOD-SCREW most often. Its deep, sharp threads wrap around a tapering shaft, and instead of pulling against a washer and nut, the woodscrew's threads cut into and pull against the wood itself. Here is the screw's great advantage: it not only fastens two pieces, but draws them together with a force multiplied by the screw machine. The screw is also far more resistant to a force pulling it directly out of its hole than the unthreaded nail.

The screw is not a simple tool, then. As a machine it is not to be beaten in, but installed. In soft pine it is sometimes possible to start a small screw with a hole made by a sharp awl or a gimlet, and to turn it in by main force. With large screws or in harder wood, however, a place must be prepared. Two holes must be drilled, three for a countersunk head. The pieces to be joined are clamped and the screw hole is begun. A twist bit drill sinks a hole as wide as the smooth shaft of the screw and as deep as the top piece of wood. A smaller twist bit drill sinks a hole as wide as the shaft of the screw inside

the threads and not quite as deep as the point in the bottom piece of wood. (The width of this smaller hole is called the root diameter.) A COUNTERSINK reams the hole to accommodate the screwhead. When the screw is turned into the hole, a countersunk head should nestle in its depression flush (even) with the surface, the smooth shaft should turn freely in its hole, and the sharp-edged threads should do the work of cutting into the wood outside the hole drilled for the taper shaft holding them. The top piece is then pulled to the bottom

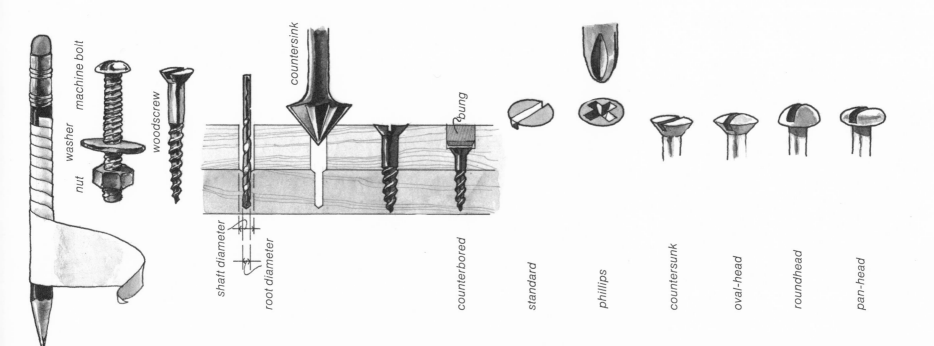

piece. The screw machine, not brute force, should do the work. If the screw is excessively hard to turn, its hole has been improperly prepared. Finish work and work exposed to weather (as in boats) have their screws sunk below the surface (counterbored) and covered by a wooden plug.

Most screwdrivers available are not ready for woodworking. The sides of their blades are not parallel and encourage the screwdriver to slip out of the screw's slot without great downward pressure. A woodworking screwdriver is filed so its faces are parallel.

But even so, the major force in driving a screw is downward into the hole, keeping the blade in the slot. Lubricating the threads by passing them lightly over a piece of soap eases the strain of turning.

There are two kinds of head slots: STANDARD, the familiar straight slot across the head, and PHILLIPS-HEAD, a cross cut into the head, requiring a different screwdriver blade. The heads themselves differ: COUNTERSUNK, ROUNDHEAD, OVAL-HEAD, and FLAT-HEAD. Woodscrews are measured by the diameter of their

shaft (given in a number between 0 and 16) and by length; a #10 x 2½ BWS cntrsk would be a number 10 shaft (about 3/16" in diameter), 2½" long, a bronze wood screw (BWS) with a countersunk head. Bronze or brass screws (sometimes chromed) are used decoratively or where there is a possibility of dampness (or in oak, where the acid nature of that wood corrodes steel screws). Steel screws are used for heavy-duty work, where hard turning might burr the soft slots of brass or bronze.

SHEET METAL SCREWS have

threads the whole length of their shaft and flat or round heads. LAG SCREWS are big steel wood screws for use in heavy timbers and are turned in with a wrench instead of a screwdriver.

41

Hides and hooves of cattle, sheep, and goats were part of a carpenter's life at one time. He boiled them down in iron pots and added whatever professional secrets he kept on his shelves to make glue. Glue, dowels, nails and screws are all parts of the handcrafter's vain, silly, beautiful hope that his work will stand up to damp, bumps, decay, scrutiny, and even Time.

Generally, glue is absorbed by both joined surfaces as it hardens. Its strength rests in the bond between its own substance and the shallow layer of wood it has penetrated. It is important, then, that the surfaces to be joined are clean—really clear of dust, grease, sweat, or anything that might hinder that absorption. Oily woods like teak should be de-greased with an agent like carbon tetrachloride. The bond is strengthened if the surfaces joined are as close as pos-sible, which usually necessitates clamping them while the glue is hard-ening.

Glue is generally not a sufficient structural fastening. It adds strength as it holds fastenings in place (like dowels), firmly beds one piece in an-other (as a tenon in a mortise), or at-taches a non-structural piece (a ve-neer table top, for example).

CASEIN GLUE is a white liquid that dries almost clear but may stain

glue

some hardwoods. It is water-based and hardens as its water evaporates into the air. It is fairly strong, but does not hold up in damp places. It is convenient, ready to squooge out of a bottle, and it is much used for interior work.

HIDE GLUE has several characteristics that has made it useful to cabinetmakers and musical instrument makers for centuries. It is made from animal parts, and comes as chunks or pellets or powders which are softened and melted over hot water. After it is spread, it cools and air-dries. It is strong but not especially weather-resistant and somewhat inconvenient.

In the matter of strength, EPOXY is unequaled. It is also completely weather-safe, and it sets (clear) chemically in a given time, independent of humidity, rain, or exposure to air. Epoxy adhesives are usually in two parts, a resin and a hardener, which are mixed in a recommended proportion and used immediately while still fluid enough to manipulate.

PLASTIC RESIN glues are packaged as dull, brown powders which change chemically when mixed with water to form a paste. They are strong, fairly weather-resistant, and they set chemically, with or without air.

ALIPHATIC RESIN glues are white, pre-mixed, strong, and weather-resistant.

CONTACT CEMENTS are usually rubber-based adhesives, and are used for sticking on a veneer (a thin sheet of wood) or plastic surfacing. It is spread on both surfaces and allowed to dry before putting the surfaces together. Contact cement is a one shot deal—make sure you position the pieces before you join them, because they will not move after they have touched.

43

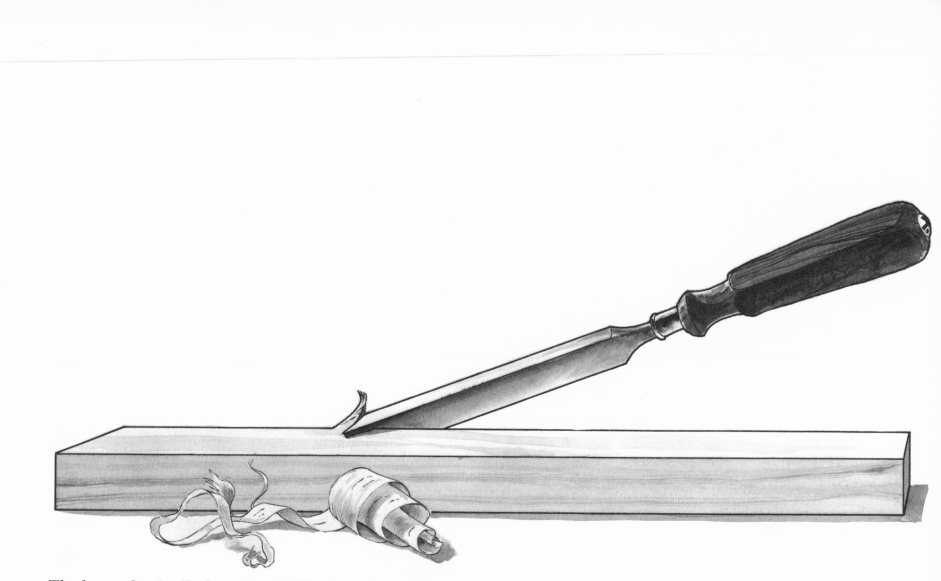

The keen edge is all of woodcraft. Wood is, after all, tough and resistant; it will try to throw your chisel off its mark, to misguide your plane. It does not want to be cut. You have a fight on your hands, and you need the sharpest tools to win well.

sharpening

INDIA COARSE

INDIA FINE   HARD ARKANSAS

You can hack a hole in a length of timber with almost anything—with a soup spoon, given time. But to cut a precise shape to exact dimensions, you need an exact edge on your tools. Preparing a tool for use is as important as using it, and a sharp tool is much easier to work with.

It is possible to sharpen a saw yourself, but it is a tedious, lengthy job, chancy for beginners. A saw sharpener will do a first-rate job for a small fee, and your saw will be sharp enough to perform surgery. You can keep your saw in good condition by keeping it away from moisture and by rubbing the blade with a cake of paraffin (not oil).

Chisel and plane irons need your own attention. Their blades want a clean,

straight edge without curves or raised parts. To work a blade down to working sharpness, the woodcrafter generally begins rough and works to smooth. He might begin with the rough side of a double-grit INDIA STONE, go to the finer side, and, if the blade must be marvelously sharp, he might use the extremely fine grit of a hard ARKANSAS STONE to polish away the marks left by the rougher stones. The scoring rough grits leave may cause the blade to wear faster.

Both a chisel and a plane iron are held as rigidly as possible in both hands or in a special tool at the cutting angle, which you can see or feel by rocking the blade slightly. This rigidity of angle is necessary to produce an even edge. The flat side of the blade is never ground,

only the bevel forming the angle of the edge.

The stone is wearing away minute bits of metal. Its pores would fill up with metal dust and stop cutting if the stone were not oiled with neat's foot, mineral, or petroleum oil. The oil floats the dust away from the cutting surface.

Stroke the blade the length of the surface in a pattern that uses the whole surface of the stone, to wear it evenly. Replace the oil pushed off and wipe the stone clean with a rough rag once in a while, replacing the oil before continuing. Use a firm, even pressure and make 25 or 50 strokes between examinations of the blade. The edge of a sharp blade will seem to disappear; it will not have glints or highlights along its extremity.

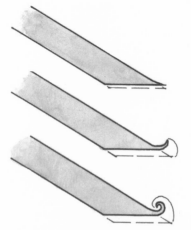

STROP

LOOK TO YOUR EDGE

Metal is formable; it can be shaped, drawn out thin, and bent. When a metal blade is being sharpened, a thin curl of metal is being formed along its edge, and this WIRE EDGE would get in the way of cutting if it were not removed. Lay the chisel or iron flat on its back, overhanging the edge of the stone, and draw it onto the face of the stone about half an inch. This will remove or loosen the wire edge and flatten the back of the edge. If the wire is not removed, the edge can be pulled across a piece of wood. When the wire is gone (you can feel it carefully with your thumb), the edge is microscopically dulled; stropping restores it. The bevel is laid on the strop and repeatedly drawn back toward the craftsman. This gentle honing reforms and polishes the edge. Though stropping is usually done on hard-tanned leather or impregnated canvas, the old timers stropped their irons and chisels on the calloused palms of their hands. The final touch, for some sharpeners, is to lightly tap the edge into a block of wood.

It is drudgery to grind a blade past a nick or dent in its edge. Always screw the plane iron back into the sole after using it, and lay a plane on its wing when you put it down to peer or measure. Chisels should be set down carefully, and rolled up in a square of heavy canvas or folded newspapers to protect their edges when transporting them.

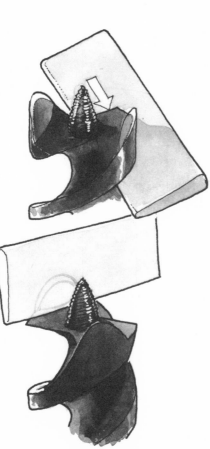

Auger bits can use a bit of sharpening before you bore away. A small file or a wedge-shaped SLIPSTONE is used to sharpen the leading edge of the spurs from the inside, and the edge of the lifting chisels from above.

Motor driven grindstones can ruin a fine edge beyond repair by nicking it, malforming it, or heating it past the point that it will retain its hardness, or temper. Handwork is the very best, here.

Hammers are almost never sharpened.

POCKET KNIFE

The Yankee boy, before he's sent to school,
Well knows the mystery of that magic tool,
The pocket-knife.

from Whittling *by John Pierpont*

index